Ready For Change?

Want To Take Charge?

Command Control?

FOLLOW ME

Alpha Dog
Don't Think, BE - Alpha Dog

Alpha Dog Training Secrets
How to Become Alpha Dog Pack Leader

By Paul Allen Pearce

PAUL ALLEN PEARCE
PUBLISHING

Copyright © 2014 Paul Allen Pearce

Look Inside!

Get Your *Free*

New Dog Training Jump Start Guide!

Learn How Your Dog Really listens and Communicates with other dogs and YOU!

"Save-Massive-Time"
Training Like a Real Pro!

Included Free

TABLE OF CONTENTS

Introduction 1

Why All the talk about Being the Alpha? 3

Is an Alpha Necessary For All Dogs? 5

Training as the Alpha 7

Who wants to be the Alpha? 12

Steps to Becoming - The Alpha 14

What Makes a Bad Alpha Leader? 33

"A Big 'Barking' Thank You!" 36

Being a Secure Alpha 37

Conclusion 38

BONUS CHAPTERS 40

Teething & Chew-Toys 40

TWO BONUS TRICKS 48

Body Language and Vocals 58

Dog Socialization 65

Handling Your Dog 75

Giving Treats 84

About the Author 91

Other Books 92

New Dog Training Jump Start Guide
<u>Before</u> You Just Go and Train Pick a Professional Trainer's Brain!
Learn Proven, Time-Saving Dog Training Success-Shortcuts

Free Thank You Gift!

Click Here to DOWNLOAD NOW!

or go to your browser and type in
http://NewDogTimes.com/Jump-Start-Guide/

New Dog Training Jump Start Guide
http://NewDogTimes.com/Jump-Start-Guide/ Free Download

Introduction

I wrote this book to inform and instruct dog owners of the fundamentals for establishing and maintaining the *alpha* position within the household hierarchy. This book is a companion book for all of my dog training books.

In the following pages you will learn how to live, lead, train, and love your dog the *alpha dog* way. Dog owners do not need to use physical intimidation to control their dogs. Non-physically assertive dominance can easily be achieved.

Leading from the *alpha* position makes everything dog related *easier*. All dogs need to know where they are positioned within the family (pack), they need to understand, and trust that their *alpha* will provide food, shelter, guidance, and affection towards them. With this method, life becomes *easier* for you and your dog.

Typically, establishing yourself as the alpha is quite easy, because after all, you are immediately feeding, caring, instructing, and loving your new dog. However, some dogs and certainly some breeds can be pushy or manipulative, and all dogs are opportunists.

The following pages will provide many helpful instructions on how to keep the relationship hierarchy intact. Boosting your leadership strength is the intention.

Science has deduced that dogs evolved from grey wolves (Canis lupus) and then over time developed into their own species. Research indicates that wolves mutated into a number of different breeds, depending upon environment, climate, and geography. Sometime between fifteen to thirty thousand years ago, they began living alongside humans in a symbiotic relationship of survival.

Given the length of time for these mutations to occur and the resulting five hundred or so unique breeds we have today, it is obvious that dogs as a species are far removed from their wolf ancestors. Dogs have evolved into their own species that led them to be the domesticated dogs we know today. Therefore, am not implying that dogs and wolves are the same.

However, some of their *primal instincts* remain imbedded into their genes. One of the most significant remaining traits is pack mentality, and inside their pack, they follow the *alpha leader.*

The facts are that dogs thrive under structure and the understanding of rules. If they know that their needs are being met by their alpha leader, they are more relaxed and at ease.

Dogs are blank slates when they enter this world. After their mother, littermates, and breeder do their minimal socialization, then the rest is up to you. If you acquire an adult dog, then you might have more of a challenge on your hands, but it is nothing that love, kindness, and direction cannot overcome while establishing yourself as the alpha leader in the family. Once you have the respect of your dog, the relationship is loving and enjoyable.

Whether you are reading this before, after, or during reading of one of my breed specific training books, I know that this information will assist and guide you while training and owning your dog.

NewPuppyStuff.com

Why All the talk about Being the Alpha?

Having the respect from the entire pack and remaining unchallenged as to who is the top dog, the undisputed leader of the pack is what all the *commotion* is.

The alpha "*walks the walk,*" and will not tolerate insubordination. The instant an alpha takes control of a pack; all in the pack must obey, or they are quickly disciplined. The *alpha* wields absolute power.

Most alpha dog's or wolves are male. This is why female dogs tend to fall into line easier. Alphas possess poise, confidence, bravery, intelligence, and self-control. An alpha does not have to be overly strong, savage, or large to be in the power seat.

To personify an alpha's attributes, they tend to hold a keen mental fortitude made up of a combination of wisdom, intelligence, and charisma, or some combination thereof that makes them good leaders allowing them to dominate. Additionally, they tend to be affectionate which makes them very good pets.

Dogs are still the only species that have allowed humans to dominate them. Dogs willingly live with humans and assist them with their lives, and a majority of cases dogs remain easygoing companions. Nonetheless, rules need to be established and enforced.

Since we were children, we have all heard the saying, "man's best friend." This saying truly fits dogs, as they are intelligent enough to take our orders but can also discern if a human deserves their respect to be the alpha of the pack.

NewPuppyStuff.com

Some breeds will absolutely challenge humans for the alpha position, which is why establishing your command early assists throughout the lifetime of your dog.

If you pay attention, you will notice that in every family there is one member above all others that the family dog respects. That person is the *alpha*, and the entire family needs to reinforce his rules and training.

The *commotion* about alpha dog status is that being the alpha keeps you in charge and respected. This allows living with your dog to be an easier and healthier arrangement.

Knowing that your dog will listen when necessary, and obey your commands will make life together less challenging and more rewarding. It is of great importance for the health and welfare of your dog, and peace of mind for the family members.

Leading as the alpha means that you are always consistent, calm, cool, and collected while enforcing rules and making corrections using a firm but fair attitude. The alpha always acts as though he or she knows that they are in charge, and is expecting to be obeyed at all times.

Additionally, the alpha shows affection and companionship. The alpha *is not* an aggressive authoritarian that doesn't have fun and play with his dogs. Instead, the alpha is the leader that is obeyed and loved by his dogs, and shows the same towards them.

NewPuppyStuff.com

Is an Alpha Necessary For All Dogs?

Regardless of the breed, your dog is seeking a leader. Giant breeds, gun dogs, herding, your dog, or the "Sir-Barks-A-lot" all need to be controlled and led by an alpha. Yep, even the little toy breeds and lapdogs need a commander. Dog owners need to guide, care, love, protect, instruct, and show affection to their dogs, furthermore, dogs seek it.

Unfortunately, many dog owners abandon their dogs. Complaints are many and vary widely, but common complaints are that their dog is "not trainable" and that "they will not obey commands."

In reality, this can be attributed to a variety of things, such as not training, not enough training, lack of consistency in rule enforcement, or no rule enforcement, and improper socialization. If any or a combination of these are not applied to your dog then it is obvious that there will be behavioral issues from the dog.

What these dog owners do not realize, is that *you* have to show dogs that you deserve their respect, loyalty, and obedience. For the entire population of those seemingly non-trainable, hyperactive, house-destroying dogs, an owner was unable to achieve the alpha position and be the leader of the pack, while additionally demonstrating a lack of willingness to engage their dogs.

It is clear that lacking interest or capability to take responsibility for dog ownership is the main culprit for most dog behavioral issues. Too many people bring home a dog when they are not equipped to be the owner that dogs deserve.

NewPuppyStuff.com

In the beginning, it takes some work to acquire the alpha mindset while adjusting to the responsibility of having a new dog. However, once achieved, keeping the position is much easier than regaining it.

Dogs need a leader to follow so they can be taught acceptable social behaviors. They are innocent to knowing what behaviors are acceptable until they are instructed. This is why early rule establishment and gently teaching and shaping their behavior to understand the rules is important.

Without a leader, they have no direction and act out their own desires. If they do this and are not disciplined they end up displaying what we call negative or unacceptable behaviors. To dogs, they are just being dogs and it is no fault of theirs because they have yet to learn proper household dog etiquette.

Dogs that will be living alongside humans must have an owner capable of being the pack-leading *alpha* they want to follow. Someone in the family needs to occupy the position, train the dog and incorporate the rest of the family into the training process so that consistency in rule enforcement can be maintained.

The result will be an obedient dog that obeys commands and rules from all family members, and well worth the effort.

Training as the Alpha

Those of you that have read one of my training books might recognize some of this brief training outline, and those that have not, should note the first sentence in the paragraphs below. I am including it as a reminder of how import the steps inside this alpha dog guide are and why they assist you in dog training and everyday life with your dog.

To begin training, establish your *alpha position* from the moment you bring your new dog or puppy home. This is done through attention, providing, scheduling, socializing, love, and using the alpha attitude.

Leading as the alpha means that you are always consistent, calm, cool, and collected while enforcing rules and making corrections using a firm but fair attitude. *The alpha always acts as though he or she knows that they are in charge.*

The best time to begin training your puppy the basics is at around six weeks to eight weeks of age. Once your puppy realizes that you control schedules, toys, mealtimes and all the things he or she cherishes, he or she will respect you as the alpha in the family hierarchy.

A positive step has been made when your puppy begins to follow you around the house. This means that he or she is bonding to you.

Remember that all family members and humans are above your dog in ranking, and should remain that way. Leading as the alpha assists you both in working together towards the goal of understanding the rules of conduct and

NewPuppyStuff.com

obedience. Your dog will be at ease when the rules are understood.

Put your puppy on a schedule for feeding, potty times, walks and play. Remain in control of toys and play time so that your dog understands that you control all good things. This is important, because if your puppy doesn't have this structure early in life, he or she will grow up thinking that they can do as they wish. No matter how wonderful and easygoing your little puppy seems now, most likely that will change with age.

Gradually begin socializing your puppy from the time you bring him or her home. Proper early socialization that continues throughout your puppy's lifetime will provide you with a well-adjusted dog that is able to handle almost any situation in a calm manner.

Early, thorough, and continual socialization is important for your dog. You do not want your dog being territorial and wary of strangers, so it is important to expose them early to a variety of situations, animals, people, and places.

Socialization benefits you and your dog by providing you both with peace of mind. With good socialization, you can expose your dog to different situations with the assurance that he or she will look to you for guidance in rules of etiquette for the indoor and outdoor world. Socialization is the foundation for all well-adjusted dogs throughout their lifetimes.

Training a dog does not suggest that your dog is supposed to only obey one master, or alpha, they must learn to obey all commands given to them by the entire family and friend circle. In essence, when you are training, and

NewPuppyStuff.com

learning to be a dog trainer, you also need to teach other family members and friends the correct way to issue these commands.

An effective incentive is to make everything you do seem fun. Always refrain from forcing your puppy to do anything they do not want to do. Highly prized treats are usually a great incentive to do something, and you will find that a fun, pleasant, friendly, happy, vocal tone combined with the treats will be ample reward for good behaviors and command compliance.

Begin training all new commands indoors. This includes silencing all of your audio-visual devices that act as distractions to dog's sensitive ears.

Training should always be an enjoyable bonding time between you and your dog. Remember that all dogs are different, and that there is no set time limit for when your dog should learn, understand, and properly obey commands.

Always have fun during training, remembering to keep your training sessions short, and stop if either of you are tired or distracted.

I always suggest beginning training new tricks or commands in an area of least distraction. I promote starting with rewards based clicker training and ending with vocal and or physical cues for your dog to follow.

If you notice any negative behavioral issues, and are not quite sure if you are offering your dog proper socialization and necessary training, do not hesitate to enter your puppy into a puppy kindergarten class to assist you with training and socialization.

Behavioral issues do not have to be present to enroll your dog into a puppy kindergarten; this assistance will benefit the both of you. Properly research the available classes so that their approach matches your own.

The time to enroll your puppy is usually around eight to ten weeks of age, and after their first round of shots, although some kindergarten classes will not accept puppies until they are three to four months of age.

Reward good behaviors, but do not reward for being cute, sweet, loveable, or huggable. If you wish to reward your dog, always reward after you issue a command and your dog obeys the command.

During your training sessions, be sure to mix it up, add a variety of toys and treats, and do not forget to have fun. Remember to provide them with ample daily exercise to keep them fit, healthy, and to keep behavioral problems away. Provide consistent structure, firm authority, rule enforcement, love and affection, and you will have one heck of a dog for you and your family.

NewPuppyStuff.com

Before We Go Any Further

– I Have a Question for you!

Did You Know That You Can Get Your **Own Breed Specific Dog Training Book**?

Look Below

GO HERE

newdogtimes.com/dog-training-books

Find Your Breed

Click the Image

Grab Your Book!

NewPuppyStuff.com

Who wants to be the Alpha?

Inside your family unit, an *alpha* needs to be chosen to lead your dog and then the entire family needs to support this family member in his or her alpha role.

In order for your dog to obey and become social, a family member needs to be the alpha your dog admires. An alpha needs to be confident, intelligent, and charismatic for commanding respect. For this reason, the other family members must never undermine the alpha's rules for acceptable dog behavior. In a sense, the rest of the family needs to act as though they are in the pack and follow the alpha's lead in any dog-related activities.

This will establish all humans above your dog in the pecking order. The other members of the family (think pack), as well as visiting friends and family, will help to reinforce and establish acceptable dog protocol. Yes, proper training and support is a group effort.

For example, let's say that your dog is trying to get your attention by nudging your hand so that you will pet him. Appropriately, you continue with your task as though he is not there. You have completely ignored him until he finally realizes that you are not going to give him attention for his nudging.

Afterward, another family member enters into the same area and your dog nudges their hand, but they give in and begin to pet and show affection. At that point, you have been *undermined* and now your dog thinks that nudging is an acceptable behavior. The result of this that he will continue to act this nudging behavior until the rest of the pack lets him know that it is not acceptable.

NewPuppyStuff.com

As I have mentioned repeatedly, the alpha is the top dog and his word needs to be the final word. This essential concept cannot be emphasized enough. The alpha needs to be above all others in the household hierarchy. He or she can still show affection, and should. The leader does not need to be mean or physically abusive.

The pack boss makes rules and is first in everything. It is understood that these rules are final. It should be made clear that the alpha will eat first, drink first, walk through doors first, leads on walks, and so forth. These rules should be adhered by the entire family and all visiting friends, therefore establishing all humans above dogs. As your dog matures and becomes obedient, these things should become natural in your dog's conduct.

Being the alpha leader means that you are in control and you maintain this control through the power of your mental abilities, *instead of from your physical responses*. You are there to gently, but firmly lead your dog into the correct direction thus shaping his behavior.

Whether it is in obedience training or socialization, vigilant and thoughtful leadership will eventually create a happy, joyful life together as your dog's master and friend.

Steps to Becoming - The Alpha

There are some steps to learn as you ascend to the top and to become the pack leader, and they consist more of mental attitude and body language rather than taking physical action. Always remember that physical punishment is not your ally but instead works against you by creating fear, resentment, and a lack of trust between you and your dog.

Being the alpha is for both of your benefits. Giving your dog a strong leader to follow makes his assimilation into your family easier and makes your life together harmonious. The list below contains the different steps you will need to master to become the top dog.

Becoming the *alpha* begins when you bring your dog home. Begin practicing the body postures, scheduling, and consistent actions from day one. Training will further allow you to begin using and showing your alpha guidance.

The commands *sit*, *stay*, and *come* are the foundation and essential fundamentals in support of you becoming the pack leader. When these commands are obeyed in any situation at a high rate of 95% or more, then you know that your dog is listening, complying, and respecting your position as the leader.

If you own a puppy, training should begin straight away. If you have a new puppy, "name recognition" is usually the first thing to teach.

Helpful Guidelines

Walk Tall

- Your body language and physical expressions should exhibit confidence and composure. Remember to maintain good posture when walking and be aware of your use of gestures and facial expressions.

- Stand tall with confidence when issuing commands, feeding, and rewarding.

- Always, maintain a higher physical position to your dog.

- At all times, use a commanding voice when administering directions to your dog. Command your dog what to do, you are not asking but telling him what to do, *so never beg your dog for a command to be completed.*

- It is important to be consistent in your behavior, and never let your dog sense that you are unsure. Continuity is essential, so remain in your alpha role at all times.

Eye Contact

- Establish eye contact with your dog and look straight at him when you are issuing a command. Do not leave room for uncertainty. Make sure that your dog senses that you are serious and should obey. No matter the dog's size, keep the eye contact.

- Before issuing a command, you must establish effective eye contact by first getting their attention by calling their name. Once you have captured their attention, you must follow up with a direct and fixed gaze into their eyes.

Be steadfast and do not let your dog look away or defy you. Maintain your stare until he or she lowers their gaze.

Your unflinching eye contact and consistent behaviors will assist your dog in sensing his or her place in the hierarchy of the family unit (pack).

Muzzle Control

- When you are handling your dog, you can use your hand to cover and hold onto their muzzle. This dominant action can be used in conjunction with the praising and loving of your dog. This is a control technique and is not used as a punishment. Please be gentle and brief when applying muzzle control. Begin with only a few seconds at first, and then build up the length of time that you can handle your dog's muzzle. For further instruction, consult the "Handling" chapter in my training books.

- It is of the utmost importance to keep your dog from biting anyone, regardless of the activity.

- Additionally, do not allow your dog to use his or her open mouth on anyone. Keeping this rule enforced is proactive training for nipping and biting behaviors.

Indifference

- If your dog enjoys meeting you at your doorway when you come home and sometimes jumps up on you or barks, simply act indifferent by ignoring him until you are ready to engage.

Continue ignoring your dog until they cease the unwanted behaviors. *Refrain from any vocal, physical and sight actions directed toward your dog.*

Always ignore your dog when he or she is acting in an annoying or unwanted way. If they have not yet learned to obey the command to "sit," or is too excited to obey, use the ignoring action. Act unaffected and not agitated until the dog stops. This avoids your command being disobeyed. More help can be found in the "Jumping" chapters of my training books.

- Guests should never be greeted first by your dog. Humans should always be the first to greet any new comers to your house. Afterwards, your guests can choose to let your dog greet or not greet.

Tight Schedule

- Remain consistent at all times, in all things that pertain to your dog. Follow a strict schedule that establishes meal times, walks, exercise/play, bathroom breaks, training sessions, and nap/sleep times.

Time continuity and routine will help your dog feel more secure and can help you in successful house breaking. By making your dog obedient to a schedule that dictates his or her routine, your dog will want to please you by following that schedule. A schedule also shows your dog that you are reliable and consistent in the care they are receiving.

Stay off My Things

- Establish your territory as being off limits to your dog.

When your dog is a puppy, make it clear that they are not allowed up on your bed. If the dog and you want to sleep close then his or her place is below your bed, in *their* bed. Use the "Off" command to keep your puppy and adult dog clear of your bed. Additionally, this is helpful for allergy sufferers and if your dog unknowingly has fleas or tick

- If you allow your dog to use any space that is private, then you will undermine your authority. If you allow them to sleep in your bed or snuggle on your couch, then they will perceive themselves as equals and free to use your private spaces at will. These spaces are yours to decide.

- Establish your areas and maintain strict enforcement, e.g. beds, couches, bedroom closet, workroom, etc. This helps to keep your dog from potentially dangerous areas in and around the house.

Establish Rank, Then Train

- Establishing alpha rank is paramount to the relationship with your dog, and it is essential in the training and life of your dog. Do not fear, it isn't that difficult when your dog is a puppy.

- The first few days after you bring your puppy home, it is essential to begin establishing the household routine for everything. Do not forget that you want your puppy to adore and trust you, so show him or her plenty of love and affection.

If your dog has not accepted you as the *Leader*, then obedience training will be difficult. When you first bring your dog home, teach a basic command such as "Sit," and this is an important part of beginning to establish yourself as the *alpha*.

If your dog begins to trail you around the house, then you are well on your way to being his or her alpha, and you can begin training sessions.

With adult dogs, training with a leash keeps you in control.

Growling is Never Allowed

- Under no circumstances are dogs allowed to growl at humans. Growling is never tolerated.

Never allow your dog to challenge you or anyone else by growling, and do not be intimidated by this action. Immediately handle any growling with a firm "No," coupled with a hand command of your choosing.

- It is essential to train your dog to understand and obey the "No" command early in his or her life. Whatever the circumstance, do not allow your puppy to growl at anyone.

- If your dog is in your arms or on the ground, reprimand him while he is down on the ground and let him know growling will not be tolerated. Be sure that you and your family are not threatened or intimidated by growling. Dogs can easily sense fear, so it is imperative that you remain steadfast in your actions.

Always, Alpha First

- Humans should always be first.

Humans should be the first through doorways, the leader on walks, the first to eat, and first at anything that you can think of. This helps maintain control of your dog, especially those large powerful breeds that like to bolt out the door and drag you with them.

- When you are passing through a doorway, be sure to hold your dog back if they are rushing to get ahead of you. Use your leash or your body, if necessary, to hold him back. You do not need to issue a command when

NewPuppyStuff.com

restraining your dog, simply hold him back behind you when entering or exiting a doorway. Once you have taught the "stay" command, you can utilize it to help set the precedent, and then later dispense with it.

If your dog manages to get in front of you, then physically move them out of the way. When humans pass through a threshold or doorway, use your command of "Stay" to keep them in place and then release them by using the command of "Come" or "Ok," after the humans have passed through the opening.

- Do not move around or step over your dog if they are blocking your way. The dog must be submissive to you and move to clear the way for you to walk. For example, if you are walking down a hallway or in the kitchen area and you encounter your dog under foot, remember that the dog moves, not you.

Stop and make sure that your dog moves aside so that you can proceed. This has a practical use, because this helps eliminate accidents such as stepping on your dog, or worse tripping and falling.

Love, Do Not Spoil

- Love but do not spoil your new puppy or dog. If you do not remain firm and consistent in commands and actions you will fail to remain in control, and there is a chance of losing your dog's respect.

For example, if you reprimand your dog for breaking a rule, don't compensate afterward by showing affection from guilt. That sends mixed signals.

- Additionally, you do not want to end up with a dog that is frightened of other dogs and humans, so *do not* over-protect your dog. Socialize your dog properly and thoroughly from puppyhood straight through the remainder of his lifetime. Expose him to the greater world.

Humans are Property Owners

- All commands of ownership need to be taught. "Drop it" and "Leave it" are two examples where a dog must leave an object alone upon your command, and of course, the all-powerful "No" can be employed, as well.

Toys, food, or whatever, should remain in human ownership. You should be able to confiscate any item, including food items from a dog without receiving a growl or aggressive behavior.

Begin this while they are puppy's and you should have little problem, but always beware that a snarl or snap is a natural reaction to stealing a dog's meaty bone that you gifted them.

Before harshly reacting, measure your own actions.

How Much and When to Pet and Coddle

- At times, when and how to show affection and love to your new puppy or dog, can be confusing.

There is nothing wrong with patting, petting, and cuddling your dog, but there are guidelines that should be followed.

- A good way to show love and affection is to issue commands that are obeyed before offering affection. Do not allow your dog to nudge you for affection, if he or she does, completely ignore them.

NewPuppyStuff.com

Command, "Sit" and after compliance, pat, pet, praise. Remember to show affection on your terms, not your dogs, and to remain physically above their head at all times.

For example, your dog comes walking up all happy and sappy seeking some attention, do not immediately squat down or take a seat and begin petting and offering your affection, instead issue the command, "Sit," then after your dog sits you can show your love.

This action is training reinforcement and your affection is the reward so it is a win-win.

Proper Handling

- Handling a puppy can be easier than an older dog. When you first get your puppy, get them used to being touched over their entire body. Roll your puppy over, rub his belly, feel his face, stick your finger in his mouth to feel teeth and gum, and handle his feet and tail.

Having your puppy or dog conditioned to this touch establishes you as alpha, but importantly it allows you to groom and inspect your dog without any uneasiness or fear on their part. These actions are also bonding actions that show you care. Furthermore, this helps them to tolerate accidental hard pats; ear or tail pulls from children, and other abnormal touching.

- If your older dog has not previously experienced this type of handling, he may not take kindly to the intrusions of touch. Go slowly and gradually increase your handling until your puppy or adult dog is used to it. They should trust you as the kind loving person that you are.

More: In **"Handling"** excerpted from my training books.

Everyone Gets R E S P E C T

- If your dog cannot overtake the alpha position from you, sometimes the dog will try to dominate other family members. Because of this potential, it is important that the entire family is capable of issuing the "Sit," "No" and "Come" commands, and that they receive obedience from your dog.

- If there is a power struggle between your dog and a family member, then have the family member take turns with the feeding and walking routines. This will show your dog that your family (humans) is also in control and are superior in ranking. Your family will need to be instructed on issuing commands that require obedience from your dog.

- Do not tolerate any insurrection toward your family and friends.

Sorry, NO Rough-housing

- Wrestling, grappling and roughhousing is outlawed in your house.

Children must refrain from contests of strength with dogs. If they are engaged, dogs will try their hardest to win, and if they do, they will think themselves the victor and that they have wrestled the alpha crown from your head.

If this happens with children, it can have some negative outcomes. You certainly do not want your dog to go around bullying your children. Explain to your family and friends that physical grappling with your dogs is off limits. You are not on a movie set where there are no consequences. This protects visitors and children from harmful injury. Rough play can escalate to heightened aggression during play.

- Common sense can be used here because casual playing often involves some grappling. However, during alpha establishment and during the initial training period, try to avoid excessive physical encounters that turn into amplified contests of strength. For safety purposes, children should always abstain.

Take all Comers

- Unwittingly, you have brought your cute little puppy home only to find out that he is an alpha. Alpha dogs make great companions. Alphas tend to be smarter, and once they have accepted you as the alpha, they are easier to train.

- You may notice that he does not listen to your commands, enjoys hopping up onto your beds and couches, and tries to enter doorways in front of you. *Do not panic*. What you have is a challenger on your hands, so keep your wits about you and enforce your will over his.

- As mentioned above, feed him and walk him on your schedule, and enforce the "you first rule" through doorways and in all other things. Stay firm, calm, confident, consistent, and enforce the rules, eventually you shall prevail, ending with you as the owner of a tremendous dog.

Keep a Keen Eye Out for Silent Takeovers

- Crafty dogs can sometimes gradually nudge you out of your alpha position without your realizing it. Be on guard for signs and symptoms that your pal is gradually pushing the boundaries and taking advantage when possible. After all, it is their instinct as opportunists, to take what they can get.

For example, you find your dog is more often on your bed and couch, and is trying to change schedules to satisfy him. If you remain alert you will not lose control, and it is a lot easier to keep it than to win it back.

"Down-Stay" Command Works

- Using the "Down" command is a great way to put your dog into a submissive posture and when coupled with "Stay," can give you some peaceful quality time while you are eating, reading, or relaxing. Once "Down-Stay" is trained, you should be able to have as much uninterrupted personal time as you wish.

- Enforce the rule that when the alpha is busy, your dog needs to remain still and quiet.

It's Not How Big You Are

- Attitude is king. Remain steadfast in all of your rules and spaces. Because you are the king or queen, do not give any leeway of control within your kingdom. The moment you falter your power will begin to shrink. Keep your bed, couch, and personal spaces for yourself only, so that your dog does not get any ideas that he or she may be able to stage a coup.

Feeding Is On Your Schedule

- You, not your dog, should dictate all feeding times and schedules. There should be no self-feeding dog feeders used. The alpha eats first and your dog must wait for you to finish. Do not feed your dog before you issue a command for him to "Sit," and he must wait patiently while you serve his food. Never allow your dog to rush in with his muzzle and start eating while you are still in process of serving.

- If your dog will not obey your commands and insists on rushing, pick up his food dish and walk away. Try feeding again later and if his attitude has not adjusted into an obeying mood repeat the same procedure of picking up his dish. Always remain standing, not kneeling when you release your dog to eat. As a reminder, issue your commands firmly and with your best alpha posture.

- When you are preparing your dog's food be watchful of your dog displaying behavior that is not calm, such as acting anxious, whining, spinning, begging, jumping, or fixing an intense gaze upon you, do not put his or her food bowl down until your dog has calmed down. You may have to correct this behavior by issuing a command such as "sit-stay." Only when your dog is calm and respectful, place the food bowl down.

- Do not feed your dog right before you are going to sit down to eat. If you feed your dog right before you sit down to eat, your dog will think that he or she is the alpha. You must be completely finished with your meal and have cleared the table before feeding your dog.

Alternatively, if your dog's usual feeding time is at least two hours before your eating time; this is enough separation so that your dog doesn't feel that he or she is the superior.

- If you have multiple dog's you must establish the pecking order beneath you and always feed your dog's according to that order.

Set the bowl down first for the dog that you choose to be directly beneath you (beta). Follow the same order each time you are *treating* your dogs.

Doing this insures that each of your dog's understands their position in the pack and keeps confusion out of the equation. You are the leader and you make the decisions and decide the pecking order. This keeps your dogs from fighting for the Beta position and other challenges amongst them.

Certain breeds do not like being subordinate to others, so before deciding, do your homework by reading and observing your different dogs so that you choose the correct pecking order.

All Treats Are Earned

- No treating unless your dog has earned and deserves it. When you are satisfied with your dog's behavior and his role inside your pack, then you may treat accordingly. Treat the same as feeding, always command a "Sit" or a different command, first, and treat after compliance.

Remember never reward misbehavior, only positive behavior. No treating your dog because he or she is cute, huggable, loveable, and your friend, ask for an action first.

- Try to avoid treating your dog when he is over stimulated and running amuck in an unfocused state of mind. This can be counterproductive and might reinforce a negative behavior resulting in you not being able to get your dog's attention.

- Some dogs have a natural gentleness to them and always take from your hand gently, while other dogs need some guidance to achieve this. If your dog is a bit rough during treat grabbing, go ahead and train the command "gentle!" when giving treats.

Be firm from this point forward. Give up no treats unless taken gently. Be steadfast with your decision to implement this, and soon your pup or dog will comply, if he wants the tasty treat.

Alpha Leads in Leash

- There is no situation where the alpha should be the one being pulled on the leash. Never should the dog be leading, tugging, or urging you forward.

When walking on the leash, your dog should remain as close to you as possible and never ahead of you. There should be slack in the leash and your dog should follow your direction changes. If he darts ahead, turn and walk the opposite direction and allow him to regain his composure. Proper leash training involving the use of the "Heel" command should keep your dog in line when you are out walking.

- Gaining your dog's attention while out walking is a great way to let him or her know that you are in charge. While on a walk have your dog heel beside you, and do not allow him to sniff, urinate, or defecate where he wishes. You are the one who chooses the spots for your dog to relieve himself.

In all cases, be sure that you lead the way and the dog is following your lead. Repeat this pack walk daily and be strict in keeping your dog's obedience to the heeling commands and sticking to the elimination rules. Having a dog that knows he must eliminate by your command makes all outings more enjoyable.

Leash training also gives both of you plenty of healthy exercise and calms your dog. Daily walks allow for practicing many commands, such as "leave it" and "no," as well as giving your dog the important daily exercise they need for their health.

Wear Him Out!

- It is good to exercise, train, and play with your dog or puppy to the point that they are worn out. Fetch games with a ball or Frisbee™ are appropriate and healthy games to play with your dog.

- At the end of the game, the ball, stick, Frisbee™, or toy always remains in your *alpha control*. Do not allow your pup or dog to run away with the ball or toy at the end of playtime.

You can also occupy his mind and body with hide and seek, agility, or scent games.

Fix All Wrongs

- As I mentioned previously, do not reward or encourage inappropriate behaviors. Some wrong behaviors are cute or silly at the time, but rewarding your dog by laughing at him while his tail is wagging with your sneaker in his mouth, are not going to work out well when one day you return home to mauled and shredded sneakers.

- It is much more difficult to fix the wrong behaviors later when he is an adult, so do it now while your dog is young and impressionable.

Lead Fairly

- Be fair and consistent in your *alpha actions*. Do not forget to balance out your run for dominance with some love and affection. Do not get lost in the leadership alpha role and forget to give affection and treats when your dog is behaving well.

Treats include praise and play. Let him know that you are happy with his behavior. This will give your dog the message that he is on the right track and behaving the way you, the leader want him to behave.

- Reward all of the appropriate behaviors, and firmly redirect when the behaviors are not wanted. Remember to keep your dominance in the middle ground, because you don't want to have a gun-shy dog, fearful of the power you wield.

Being calm, firm, intelligent, loving, and composed, will allow you to lead, and as a result, your dog will follow. No matter how tough or stubborn your dog, he will fall in line if you follow these guidelines.

With the proper attitude and training, you can have the satisfaction of having one of those dogs that follow your every command, obeys every vocal and hand signal, and enjoys doing it!

Listen to your intuition and use sound judgment in following these guidelines. Use what you need for your dog. Maybe your dog is already an easy-going relaxed dog that obeys your commands and follows your rules. If this is the case then some of these guidelines may not be necessary for you to have a mutually respectful relationship.

Thank YOU! with a very Special, Free Gift!

Hi, it's me '*Paul*' (Author, and 'new friend' I hope:)

Below is a picture of me during a family trip to Thailand. If you have never been, make plans to go, it is beautiful. My kids and I sure missed our dogs and we couldn't wait to get home and hug them. I mean WOW! What an impact our dogs have in our everyday love, family bonding; and happiness.

The reason we share this powerful bond is the information inside the unique Jump Start Guide that includes effective ways to understand, care and communicate with my dogs at a much higher level. The benefits and rewards of owning a dog are too many to mention here. ☺ I described my own personal favorites above ☺.

Thank you for trusting me to guide you so that you experience the same happiness and peace of mind my family enjoys with our dogs. Now you too can experience that same joy! Download it today!

> Please Accept my **Free Thank You Gift** !
> the
> "New Dog Training Jump Start Guide"

and
DOWNLOAD
Your Free Gift Copy - Below -Today!

"Click it" to:

"The lasting benefits you TOO can experience, will go WAY beyond the professional knowledge you will learn!"

Thanks Again!
~Paul

> # DOWNLOAD it HERE!

Or You Can Type This Address In Your Browser:
www.newdogtimes.com/jump-start-guide/

NewPuppyStuff.com

What Makes a Bad Alpha Leader?

Excessive Toughness

- Be firm, but not oppressive.

- Never lash out because you are in a bad mood or are angry. Be firm when your dog is not obedient.

- Only discipline when absolutely necessary, and do it an appropriate non-abusive manner, which excludes physical pain and refraining from a tyrannical vocal rage.

Keep in your forethoughts that you are shaping behavior, and your dog will learn there are consequences to his negative behaviors. The goal is to avoid your dog fearing you. Fear creates its own set of emotionally and possibly physical consequences.

Indecisive and Erratic Discipline

- Remain consistent in disciplining and rewarding. If you are not they will sense the weakness and try to leverage it. Consistency is paramount in maintaining your position as the alpha, training, and all dog-related matters. They appreciate it.

- *Consistency avoids confusion*. If you do not discipline in the same manner for a negative behavior, then the mixed signals confuses dogs.

This pertains to clicking at the right moment, rewarding at the right moments, and always acting with confidence instead of timidity.

Physical Discipline

NewPuppyStuff.com

- Physical discipline is not recommended. Using this type of discipline has been shown to make dogs less obedient. This type of discipline instills fear into your dog, and can possibly increase or promote stubbornness.

- Physical discipline also causes dogs to act out many negative, some serious behavioral issues and potentially mentally damage a dog. Dogs can become listless, avoid human contact, lose vibrancy, and attempt to do the least expected from them in order to avoid punishment.

Equal treatment

- If you treat your dog as an equal, you will undermine your own authority as the *alpha,* and open yourself to being challenged.

Solitary Confinement for Wrong Behavior

- This can be severe for some dog breeds, especially dogs that are more pack and family oriented.

Time outs are good for short-term punishments for very bad behaviors, but long isolation can be psychologically damaging.

- If isolation is administered for barking, howling, or destructive behavior, it may reinforce rather than modify the undesired behaviors. Fix the behavior, and do not be afraid to solicit help from professionals or friends.

- *Avoid using your dog's crate for time-outs. Instead, find a dull boring area.*

Loss of Control

- Alpha's are always in control of their emotions and actions. These attributes are part of the recipe for being a good leader. If you lose your temper and lash out verbally or physically, it will not work in your favor.

- I realize this can be difficult, especially if your dog is in danger or endangering others, but as a rule try to maintain that alpha calm, cool, collected behavior.

You may have noted that the role of being the alpha is about maintaining an attitude that encourages your dog to pay quick attention to you. Your dog's obedience to your commands concurrently offers you respect and love that an alpha deserves.

It is not power that comes from physical dominance, but instead it is mental confidence, fortitude, and consistency of attitude that always reveals that there are no doubts you are in command, and must be obeyed.

This attitude must be acted out daily, without fail, for the life of your dogs. You are responsible for all of your dog's needs. You will groom, walk, love, aid, and teach him as you lead him down the path of socialization and obedience. As the alpha, you take full responsibility for his complete well-being.

Are you up to the task? I think you will be just fine. We all want a loving obedient dog. The alpha acts as an alpha because he wants the best for his dog, knowing that he can bear the responsibility.

NewPuppyStuff.com

"A Big 'Barking' Thank You!"

Did you know that underneath my shaggy brown hair, that there are two gigantic ears for listening?

Can you please help tell me if I helped you to

become an alpha dog?

Do you understand what being the alpha entails?

Please Tell Me with a *Quick*

and

Positive Review Here

amazon.com/dp/B00ICGQO40

- *Thank you very much for all of your help in helping me, and others!*

~ *Paul*

NewPuppyStuff.com

Being a Secure Alpha

Start by being a loving alpha and always act from a place of love. Know yourself and your dog. Dogs are smart and you must prove that you are at a level above them and deserving of their respect.

This is not that difficult because you have many IQ points above them, but your physical and emotional actions are quickly sensed by them. These human attributes are a bit more difficult for us to regulate and hide from their keen senses. That is not always bad, because they know when to comfort you.

Begin by learning the things that your dog does and does not like, their body language, fears, and what makes them happy. Be consistent with reprimands and love. *Good timing* will keep your dog from getting confused as to which behavior is being disciplined, or rewarded. *Timing is crucial in dog training.*

Remember to be your dog's rock. Be fair, consistent, trustworthy, patient, and confident in providing everything he needs. Consistently displaying these traits will show your dog that you are capable of leading and taking care of him. You might think this is common sense, but you also might be surprised at how many people do not act this way towards their dogs.

I know you possess the skills and love that will make you a great pack leader, or you would not have brought your dog home and be reading this book.

Conclusion

Have you been implementing these steps? Did you gain strength in your alpha position? Did you learn some information that helped you demand your dog's respect? I hope that the answer is yes to all of the above.

I realize that some dog owners enjoy having their dog's lounge on couches or beds while sharing their close companionship, and heck, it is common practice. Unfortunately, it is not a good thing to do when you are establishing your alpha position, defining rules, shaping, and training your dog into an obedient dog that adores his master and understands the rules. Of course, later you can adjust your attitude to what you are comfortable.

As a solution, implementing commands that allow your dog to get up onto normally off-limits objects or places can be implemented.

If you decide to allow your dog on beds and couches with you, always keep your head and shoulders above your dog. Be confident that when you command "off," your dog immediately replies. Practice the *off* command frequently.

Go with the flow; enjoy all of the steps in dog ownership and remain lighthearted. Dogs are wonderful to have around and to accompany you on hikes, camping, or during exercises. Personally, I could not imagine a world without dogs. They bring great comfort, laughs, assistance, and fun to the human experience. They truly are a blessing and natural pairing to us, the two-legged upright walker.

There will be times when all of the things that I have listed in this alpha guide will occur, but now you know to recognize actions that can potentially undermine your

NewPuppyStuff.com

alpha position and affect your relationship with your dog. Remain diligent and you will maintain your position as the alpha leader and thus partake of the positive outcome.

My mission is that you and your dog have a mutually respectful relationship that has your dog always looking to you for guidance because he respects you as the leader.

Next, I have included some bonus materials from my training books that will aid you in the training and care of your dog.

~ Paps

BONUS CHAPTERS
Teething & Chew-Toys

Between the third and sixth week your puppy will begin to feel the notorious baby teeth eruption. Puppy teeth are not designed to grind heavy foods, and consist of predominantly small, razor sharp canines and incisors. These new teeth number about twenty-eight, and during this painful and frustrating teething period, puppies will attempt to seek relief on anything within reach that they can clamp their little mouths down on.

Later, when the baby teeth fall out and their adult teeth emerge, this will again cause discomfort, further increasing their drive to chew in search of relief. Usually by the end of six months, the intense chewing phase begins to wane. Although some variance exists by breed, adult dogs have forty-two teeth with the molars coming in last at around six to seven months of age.

Puppies are motivated to chew because of the discomfort that comes from teething, as well as to investigate new objects of interest. Chewing is a normal dog behavior that can be steered and directed toward owner approved toys and objects. Dogs certainly love to chew on bones, and they can spend hours gnawing until they feel that they have successfully scoured it clean, sometimes burying it for a later chew session, or solely as a trophy. Wood, bones and toys are some of the objects that occupy a dog during the activity of chewing.

Chewing not only provides stimulation and fun, but it serves to reduce a dog's anxiety. It is our job to identify what our puppies can and cannot chew on, while gently establishing and enforcing the rules of chewing. This process begins by providing an ample amount of chew-toys for our puppy.

Chew-toys

A non-edible chew-toy is an object made for dogs to chew that is neither, consumable or destructible. Non-food items eaten by dogs are dangerous and can sometimes seriously harm your dog, so it is imperative to provide high quality and durable chew-toys.

Choosing the type of chew-toy will depend upon your dog's individual preferences and chewing ability, so you may have to go through several to find the most appropriate. Some *super chewer* dogs can destroy a rawhide chew in a fraction of the time as others, so your dog's prowess and jaw power will dictate the types of chews that you will want to provide.

Edible chews such as pig ears, rawhide bones, Nylabones®, and other natural chew products are also available and appropriate for your puppy or adult dog. Beware that sometimes edibles can come apart in large chunks or pieces, thus having the potential to be swallowed, or possibly choke a dog. For safety, keep an eye on your dog whenever he is working away on an edible chew. While your puppy is discovering the variety and joy of chewing, take notice of the chews that he enjoys most.

KONG® and Petsafe® make plenty of top quality chew-toys, including those can be stuffed with food, such as kibble or cheese, to hold your dog's interest. KONG® products as well as the Petsafe® Busy Buddy® line are

NewPuppyStuff.com

made from natural rubber and have a stellar reputation for durability.

Many other brands are available to choose. When choosing chew-toys, take into consideration whether or not you are purchasing a natural or synthetic product, as well as keep in mind what your pal's preferences are. Usually, anything that you stuff with food will begin a puppy craving for that particular toy, but be aware that is not always the case.

Stuffing Chew-Toys

There are some basic guidelines to follow when using a stuffable chew toy. First, kibble is the recommended foodstuff when filling your puppy's chew-toy. Kibble assists in keeping your puppy at a normal weight, and if this is a concern, you can simply exclude the amount you used in the toy from his normal feeding portion.

Secondly, you can use tastier treats, such as cooked meat or freeze-dried liver, but these should be reserved for special rewards. There are plenty of stuffing recipes available, but be cautious about the frequency you treat your puppy with special stuffing.

Be conscious of when you reward your puppy, and avoid doing so when bad behaviors are exhibited. For example, if your puppy has been incessantly barking all afternoon, then if you provide a stuffed chew-toy do not reward him with something utterly delectable.

The art to stuffing chew-toys is that the toy holds your puppy's interest, and keeps him occupied. For your success, you will want to stuff the toy in a way that a small portion of food comes out easily, thus quickly rewarding

NewPuppyStuff.com

your puppy. After this initial jackpot, the goal is to keep your puppy chewing while gradually being rewarded with small bits of food that he actively extracts. You can use a high value treat, such as a piece of meat stuffed deeply into the smallest hole, which will keep your dog occupied for hours in search of this prized morsel.

With a little creativity and practice, the art of chew-toy stuffing will be acquired benefitting you and your canine friend. After trial and error, you will begin to understand what fillings and arrangements will keep your puppy occupied for longer and longer times.

Why Feed Dinner from Stuffed Chew-Toys?

Here is some advice that I gleaned off a friend of mine, and it does seem to pack some merit. As you are probably aware, the current practice indicates that puppies should be fed two to three times daily, from their bowl. There is nothing wrong with this, but it does raise a question as to whether perhaps they think that they are being rewarded for the non-acceptable behaviors that was possibly acted just prior to eating time. This should be taken into consideration, and feeding should be adjusted to avoid potential negative behavior reinforcement.

The other item that I was made aware is that if you feed your puppy by stuffing his chew-toy, it will occupy more of his time and keep him from negatively acting out of boredom, excessive curiosity, or abundant adrenal stores.

The argument against bowl feeding is that it supplants the activity of searching for food, as they would in the wild, and as a result of the quick gratification in the easy meal, there remains an over-abundance of time remaining to satisfy the dog's mental and physical stimulation.

To understand this better you have to put yourself into a puppy's paws. Besides sleeping and training, your dog has about twelve hours each day to fill with satisfying and rewarding activity. Resulting from an excess of unoccupied time, normal behaviors, such as grooming, barking, chewing, walking, and playing can become repetitive and unfulfilling. Sometimes an activity can lose its initial purpose and meaning, only to become a way to pass time instead of serving as a positive function of daily life. Obsessive and compulsive behaviors can come out of these long sessions of boredom. For example, vocalizing for alarm can become ceaseless barking, and grooming can turn into excessive licking or scratching, likely resulting in harm to the skin.

It falls upon us to instruct our puppies on healthy, calm and relaxing ways to pass the time of day. This is a critical part of training and socialization. Remember, that by stuffing the chew-toy full of kibble you can successfully occupy hours of your puppy's time, helping to reduce the possibility of negative behaviors overtaking your puppy.

This can be accomplished by redirecting his attention to an activity that he enjoys, keeping his mind distracted from the potential of loneliness and boredom. Because of his time spent chewing the approved toy, he is kept calm and his time occupied, periodically rewarded by bits of kibble, and thus the possibility of developing any of the potential, aforementioned negative behaviors is minimized.

NewPuppyStuff.com

This feeding option is a method originally suggested by Dr. Ian Dunbar, a famed rewards-based trainer and SIRIUS® puppy-training pioneer. However, this method is not essential to maintain and train a healthy puppy; I felt it was worth mentioning since I was writing about chew-toys.

Many people refrain from feeding their dog's kibble, utilizing the optional diet of raw foods, thus modification in the feeding method would be required here. Other factors when utilizing this method should take into consideration your dog's individual personality, as well as ability to withdraw food from the toy. Whichever feeding method you choose to use, be certain to feed your puppy the healthiest, least processed, non-chemical laden foods that you can find.

Bones

Later, as your puppy grows he will no doubt be interested in other types of things to chew on, as well as to eat. There exists some controversy as to whether raw bones, cooked bones, or any animal bones are at all good for dogs to chew. I do not want to state with certainty that bones are safe for your dog, as there is some obvious risks involved, but I do feed my dogs bones without problem.

As a new dog owner, and with time and assessment, you can later determine what is best for your dog. Any concerns that surface can be solved by consulting your veterinarian, speaking with your breeder, and of course making a decision based upon your own findings and personal experience.

Recommendations are to provide your dog with bones that are sold specifically for chewing, which are often beef, or bison femur or hipbones, filled with satisfying marrow. Chicken bones and steak bones that have been cooked can splinter and pose a greater choking risk and should not be given to your dog.

Some dogs that are intense chewers often chip a tooth, or splinter small pieces off the bones they are gnawing at, and because of this, it is good to supervise them. Be sure to avoid small bones in favor of larger raw bones. Present the bones on an easy to clean surface or somewhere outdoors. If you have more than one dog, it is important to separate them to avoid conflict. Also, be aware that dogs not who are not used to the rich, high calorie marrow inside of these bones could possibly have a bout of diarrhea after consumption.

Health Insurance for my Dog?
Really? Why?

Because Paying Cash Makes No "Cents" or Does It?
Shocking Statistics! **Discover the Truth!**

healthypaws
PET INSURANCE & FOUNDATION

Protect Your Pet.
Save a Homeless Pet.

TRUSTED BY PET PARENTS & LOVED BY PETS!

Protect your best friend and save on vet bills!

- ☑ Lifetime discounts up to 10%
- ☑ Unlimited Benefits
- ☑ #1 Customer-Rated Plan

Quote and Save

~ **Type Into Your Browser**

nobrainerdogtrainer.com/insurance-for-dogs

NewPuppyStuff.com

TWO BONUS TRICKS
The "Sit" Command

"Sit" is one of the basic commands that you will use regularly during life with your dog. Teaching your puppy to *sit* establishes human leadership by shaping your dog's understanding of who the boss is. This command can also help curb problem behaviors, such as jumping up on people. It can also assist in teaching polite doggy etiquette, particularly of patiently waiting for you, *the trusted alpha.* Teaching your dog to sit is easy, and a great way for you to work on your catalog of essential alpha behaviors touched upon in previous chapters.

- First, gather treats, then find a quiet place to begin the training. Wait until your puppy sits by his own will, and soon as his fuzzy rump hits the floor, *click and treat*. Treat your pup while he is still sitting, then promptly get him up and standing again. Continue doing this until your pup immediately sits back down in anticipation of the treat. Each time he complies, be sure to click and treat.

- Next, integrate the verbal command of "sit." Each time he begins to sit on his own, say, "sit," then reinforce with a C/T. From here on, only treat your pup when he sits after being commanded to do so. Practice for 10-15 repetitions then take a break.

Try these variations for better sitting behavior:

- Continue the training by adding the distraction of people, animals, and noises to the sessions. As with the come command, you want your dog to sit during any situation

NewPuppyStuff.com

that may take place. Practice for at least five minutes each day in places with increasingly more distractions.

- Run around with your dog while you are sharing play with one of his favorite toys. After getting him worked up and excited, command your dog to *sit*. Click and treat your dog when he does.

- Before going outside, delivering food, playing with toys, giving verbal praise, petting, or getting into the car, ask your dog to *sit*. Having your dog sit before setting his food bowl down is something you can practice every day to help bolster his compliance to the sit command.

- Other situations where you can practice the sit command can be when there are strangers present, or before opening doors for visitors. In addition, other excellent opportunities to work on the sit command is when there is food on the table, when you are barbequing, or when you are together in the park.

Keep practicing this command in all situations that you may encounter throughout the day with your dog. I recommend a gradual increase to the level of distraction exposure during this training. Sit is a powerful and indispensable command that you will utilize throughout the life of your dog. Later, we will add the command of "sit-stay" in order to keep your dog in place until you release him.

-It is important eventually to phase out the clicking and treating every time that he obeys the "sit" command. After his consistent obedience to the command, you can begin gradually to reduce C/T by treating every other compliance, then once out three times, followed by once out of four, five, six, and then finally cease.

Be sure to observe your dog's abilities and pace, making sure not to decrease C/T too rapidly. The overall goal of this training is to have your dog obey all commands without a reward, and only by a vocal or physical cue.

-Take advantage of each day, and the multiple opportunities you have to practice the sit command.

Excerpted from Paul's "49 ½ Dog Tricks" book, which will be published soon.

Introduction

Did you ever want to amaze and entertain your friends and family with the type of dog that can, will, and wants to do anything at any time, a show-off dog? You know that dog that understands vocal and body signals, reacts when commanded, and is a great companion in life.

The tricks inside this book are the kind of fun and useful tricks that can give you that kind of dog when together you master them. After training these tricks included inside this book, you and your dog can have a joyful and fruitful life together as friends and partners in showmanship.

Trick #14 Teaching Release

Release has an easy rating and requires that your dog knows the sit and stay commands. The supplies needed are your clicker, and some treats.

I use "rise" to release my dog Jake, but there is nothing wrong with using *release, move, break*, or a simple word that you feel comfortable using. Try to avoid yes, okay, and other commonly used words that are used in everyday conversation.

This command informs your dog that they are free to move from whichever previous command you had issued and your dog complied, such as *sit, down*, or *stay*. It does not imply that your dog is free to run off and play on his own. It is specifically for your dog to stand up and prepare for the next command.

NewPuppyStuff.com

Release is easier to train if your dog already *sits* and *stays* on command. If you have told your dog to stay, he will sit patiently and he should remain in the sitting position until released. This is an obedience command that can keep your dog safe and you from worrying about your dog bolting off or moving at the wrong time, and it is an easy way to let your dog know when it is acceptable for him to move.

The goals for your dog to learn are that other movements besides the release cues are not a cue to move, your dog gets up or moves immediately when you command, and your dog stays put until the command *release* is given, and besides standing up, your dog does no other actions. When successfully trained your dog will ignore all other movements and words and will release only when the proper vocal or hand signal is used.

If your dog gets up *without* the release command, *do not* click and treat. When your dog regularly obeys release, you will have greater control over your dog. This reinforces that you are the leader and in control at all times.

Do not move forward to the next step until your dog is regularly obeying the step that you are working.

1. Begin training in a quiet place with few distractions, and bring plenty of treats.

2. Select a hand signal that is not associated with another command, and that you will use in conjunction with the vocal command "release."

3. Say the command "down" to your dog. After he obeys and is in the down position, give an internal count of around three seconds, when the time is up;

NewPuppyStuff.com

simultaneously issue the vocal command "release" and your hand signal. If your dog does not rise put some enthusiasm into your voice and hand signal and your dog should release, then when he does, *click and treat*. Then directly afterward command your dog back into the down position and C/T. Continue repeating until your dog upon command is regularly releasing from the down position. Gradually increase the time between the *down* command and *release* command from three to ten seconds. Repeat 6-10 times per session depending upon your dog's attention.

4. After using the excited voice and hand gesture, we will move to the vocal command and hand gesture but this time begin gradually decreasing your enthusiasm and moving towards using your normal command tone voice. Give an internal count of around ten seconds, when the time is up; simultaneously issue the vocal command "release" with your hand signal, C/T when he does. Then directly afterward command your dog back into the down position and C/T.

Continue repeating until your dog upon command is regularly releasing from the down position. Repeat 6-10 times per session. Continue practicing until your dog will release when you use your normal command voice without elaborate enthusiasm or excess gestures.

5. Next, cease using the hand gesture and only use your vocal command saying "release," and when your dog does, C/T. As you practice, gradually put less enthusiasm into your voice command until you arrive at your normal command voice. Start by issuing the command "down," count off five seconds and then use only the vocal command when releasing. Then directly afterward command your dog back into the down position and C/T.

Continue repeating until your dog upon command is regularly releasing from the down position. Before moving to step six, gradually increase the down-release time to 10-15 seconds. Repeat 6-10 times per session.

6. Practice the release command from the sit and down positions. Later, increase the time between your commands sit, down, stay, and issuing the release command. You want your dog to feel relaxed and good about waiting to move, and follow your next command. Increase the time that your dog stays using increments of three to five seconds per session, and when your dog becomes used to staying for longer, you can increase the increments to whatever time you and your dog are comfortable.

Eventually you want to arrive at the place where your dog will stay for fifteen minutes or longer.

During the time increment increases, also increase the distance between you and your dog while your dog is in the down position. Gradually begin moving further away from your dog before issuing the vocal release command. *Go to where your dog has risen and C/T where he is standing, do not have him come to you for the treat.*

7. Next, practice this in a variety of areas and in situations of various distraction. After success indoors and outdoors in your yard, then wander into the neighborhood, and beyond. Remain patient in the more distracting locations and gradually increase the amount and types of distractions. Distractions can also include his toys be tossed or played with.

- Check how your dog reacts when you grab his favorite ball or tug. Does he stay in place or rise up to play? He should remain in the down position that you had him commanded.

- If other distractions are occurring and your dog stays in the down position, give your dog a C/T for remaining down. If you notice that your dog is restless due to surrounding distractions, give a C/T while the distraction is occurring and after the distraction has ended. These reward reinforcements will help your dog understand that he is being rewarded for remaining in the positon that you requested.

- Mix up the treats and time increments so that your dog never knows when the reward or which treat is coming next.

Gradually phase out clicking and treating your dog every time that he obeys the release command. Reduce the treats to one time out of two compliances, followed by one out of three, then one out of four, five, six, and finally stop altogether.

Do not decrease the treats too rapidly and be sure to observe closely, your dog's abilities and pace. The goal of the training is to have your dog obey *all* commands with only a vocal or physical cue, *without a reward*.

Hands On

The release that I taught Jake was "rise" Whenever I said "rise" Jake knew that he was free to stand up from the previous command *down*. Additionally, I use this command daily to keep him sharp. It is useful when I need him still for just a few minutes or longer while I do something. It also helps me when I want Jake to standby while I open the truck door. I say "sit," then when I am ready "rise," followed by "up" and he jumps into the truck.

Troubleshooting

My dog has ZERO patience and releases on his own clock!

This is shared with all dogs until they get used to the command. Your dog may be anticipating the count between the "down" command and the release, a solution to this is to change up the time between the command and release, such as four seconds then seven seconds the next. Another thing that humans do is give physical cues that they are not aware.

 A simple raised eyebrow or slight hand movement maybe triggering a perceptive dog to release. Later these other cures will gradually be trained away, so that your dog will only obey the release vocal or hand cue.

Hint: Always remain positive and excited. This will help your dog learn this trick. In training, we have to keep our frustrations hidden from dogs. Vocal, facial, physical movements and tones need to remain consistent during training.

If you are frustrated or tired, finish the session on a high note and start again later or another day. There is no hurry for you or your dog to learn tricks.

NewPuppyStuff.com

Before We Go Any Further – I Have a Question for you!

Did You Know That You Can Get Your **Own Breed Specific Dog Training Book**?

Look Below

GO HERE

newdogtimes.com/dog-training-books

Find Your Breed

Click the Image

Grab Your Book!

NewPuppyStuff.com

Body Language and Vocals

Training your dog seems like a daunting task, but it is a unique and rewarding experience. It is the foundation of a healthy and long relationship with your new dog or puppy. You must be the one in charge of the relationship and lead with the pack leader mentality, all the while showing patience and love.

Without a doubt, it is nice to have an obedient friend by your side through good times and bad. Owning a dog is a relationship that needs tending throughout the years. Once you begin training, it will continue throughout the life of your dog and friend. An obedient dog is easier to care for and causes less household problems and expense. You know what needs to be done, but what about your dog. How do you read his messages in regards to what you are attempting to accomplish? I am going to cover dog's body language and vocal language to provide insight into what it is your dog is trying to tell you. This should prove to be an asset while training your dog.

Remember that we cannot always read a dog's body language accurately. All dogs have their own unique personality; therefore will express themselves in their individual way. It is possible that a dog's happy wagging tail could be another dog's way of conveying that it is nervous or anxious. Keep in in your thoughts when reading a dog's body language that it is difficult to be 100% accurate interpreting and to use caution around strange dogs.

Body Language:

What is body language? Body language is all of the non-verbal communication we exhibit when engaged into an exchange with another entity. Say what? All of those little tics, spasms, and movements that we act out comprise of non-verbal body language. Studies state that over 50% of how people judge us is based on our use of body language. Apparently, the visual interpretation of our message is equal to our verbal message. It is interesting how some studies have indicated that when the body language disagrees with the verbal, our verbal message accounts for as little as 7-10% of how the others judge us. With that kind of statistic, I would say that body language is extremely important.

Similar to humans, dogs use their bodies to communicate. Their hearing and seeing senses are especially acute. Observe how your dog tilts his head, moves his legs, and what is his tail doing while you are engaged. Is the tail up, down, or wagging? These body movements are all part of the message your dog is trying to convey. With this knowledge, I think it is safe to say that we should learn a little about human and dog body language. In this article, I will stick to a dog's body language and leave the human investigation up to you. What do you think my posture is right now?

The Tail:

The tail is a wagging and this means the dog is friendly, or maybe not. With most dogs that have tails it can convey many messages, some nice, some nasty. Specialists say a dog's wagging tail can mean the dog is scared, confused, preparing to fight, confident, concentrating, interested, or happy. Some dogs have curly spitz type tails and therefore

NewPuppyStuff.com

it will take a keen eye to see and denote what their tail position might be conveying so you will have to rely more on facial and body postures. Breeds with docked tails, flat faces, and that are black in color make it more difficult to read what they are trying express. From distance black colored dogs facial expressions can be difficult to see. Creating further difficulties are breeds that have puffy hair, long hair, or extensive hair that hides their physical features.

How do you tell the difference? Look at the speed and range of motion in the tail. The wide-fast tail wag is usually the message of "Hey, I am so happy to see you!" wag. The tail that is not tight between the hind legs, but instead is sticking straight back horizontally means the dog is curious but unsure, and probably not going to bite but remain in a place of neutral affection. This dog will probably not be confrontational, yet the verdict is not in. The slow tail wag means the same; the dog's friendly meter is gauging the other as friend or foe.

The tail held high and stiff, or bristling (hair raised) is a WATCH OUT! - Red Flag warning for humans to be cautious. This dog may not only be aggressive, but dangerous and ready to rumble. If you come across this dog, it is time to calculate your retreat and escape plan.

Not only should the speed and range of the wag be recognized while you are reading doggie body language, one must also take note of the tail position. A dog that is carrying its tail erect is a self-assured dog in control of itself. On the other side of that, the dog with their tail

NewPuppyStuff.com

between their legs, tucked in tight is the, "I surrender man, I surrender, please don't hurt me" posture.

The chill dog, "a la Reggae special" is the dog that has her tail lowered but not tucked in-between her legs. The tail that is down and relaxed in a neutral position states, the dog is relaxed.

While training your dog or simply playing, it is a good idea to take note of what his or her tail is doing and determine if your dog's tail posture is matching their moods. Your understanding of your dog's tail movements and body posture will be of great assistance throughout its lifetime.

Up Front:

On the front end of the dog is the head and ears with their special motions. A dog that cocks his head or twitches her ears is giving the signal of interest and awareness, but sometimes it can indicate fear. The forward or ear up movements can show a dog's awareness of seeing or hearing something new. Due to the amazingly acute canine sense of hearing, this can occur long before we are aware. These senses are two of the assets that make dogs so special and that make them fantastic guard and watchdogs.

"I give in, and will take my punishment" is conveyed with the head down and ears back. Take note of this submissive posture, observe the neck, and back fur for bristling. Sometimes this accompanies this posture. Even though a dog is giving off this submissive stance, it should be approached with caution because it may feel threatened and launch an offensive attack thinking he needs to defend himself.

"Smile, you are on camera." Yep, you got it, dogs smile too. It is usually a subtle corner pull back to show the teeth. Do not confuse this with the obvious snarl that entails a raised upper lip and bared teeth, sometimes accompanied by a deep growling sound. The snarl is something to be extremely cautious of when encountered. A snarling dog is not joking around--*the snarl is serious*. This dog is ready to be physically aggressive.

The Whole Kit and Caboodle:

Using the entire body, a dog that rolls over onto its back and exposes his belly, neck, and genitals is conveying the message that you are in charge. A dog that is overly submissive sometimes urinates a small amount to express his obedience towards a human or another dog.

Front paws down, rear end up, tail is a waggin.' This, "hut, hut, hut, C'mon Sparky hike the ball," posture is the ole K-9 position of choice for, "Hey! It is playtime, and I am ready to go!" This posture is sometimes accompanied with a playful bark and or pawing of the ground in an attempt to draw you into his playful state. I love it when a dog is in this mood, albeit they can be aloof to commands.

Whines, Growls, Howls, Barks and Yelps. Sounds dogs make and we hear

We just had a look at the silent communication of body language. Now, I will look into the doggie noises we cherish, but sometimes find annoying. Just what is our dog trying to tell us? Our canine friends often use vocal expressions to get their needs met. Whines and growls mean what they say, so when training your dog, listen carefully. As you become accustomed to the dogs vocal communication, and are able to begin understanding them, the happier you will both become. Some dog noises can be annoying and keep you awake, or wake you up. This may need your attention, to be trained out as inappropriate vocalizations.

Barking:

What does a dog bark say and why bark at all? Dogs bark to say "Hey, what's up dude," "I am hungry," or "Look at me!" A bark may warn of trouble, or convey that the dog is bored or lonely. I think we all know that stimulated and excited dogs also bark. It is up to us to survey the surroundings and assess the reason. We need to educate ourselves about our dog's various barks so we can act appropriately.

Whining and Whimpering:

Almost from the time they are freshly made and feeding upon their mother's milk, our little puppies begin to make their first little fur-ball noises. Whimpering or whining to get their mothers attention for feeding or comfort is innate, and as a result, they know mom will come to them. They also use these two W's on us to gain our attention. Other reasons for whimpering or whining are from fear produced by loud noises such as thunderstorms or fireworks. I think most of us have experienced the 4th of July phenomenon where the entire dog population is barking excessively until the wee hours of the morning when the last fireworks are ignited, and the final "BOOM!" dies off.

Growling:

NewPuppyStuff.com

Growling means, you had better watch out. Be acutely aware of what this dog is doing or might do. Usually a dog that is growling is seriously irritated and preparing to be further aggressive. However, this is not always true, sometimes a dog will issue a growl requesting for petting to continue.

Howling:

Picture the dark silhouette of a howling dog with a full moon backdrop. A dog's howl is a distinct vocalization that most dogs use, and every wolf makes. Howling can mean loneliness, desire, warning, or excitement. A lonely howl is a dog looking for a response. Dogs also howl after a long hunt when they have tracked and cornered their prey. Some Scenthounds use a distinct sound named a bay.

More inside the New Dog Starter Guide!

http://newdogtimes.com/jump-start-guide/

Dog Socialization

What, Where, When, Why

To understand the importance of socialization, and why it is regularly mentioned by dog trainers, let us begin by looking at how a puppy's social development process is played out from puppy to adulthood.

Dog socialization is learning and maintaining acceptable behavior in any situation, especially when the dog or puppy does not want too. The goal is learning to handle any normal experience that occurs in life without becoming overly stimulated, fearful, reactive, or aggressive. The goal is that no matter what the circumstance; your dog is able to go with the flow, keep centered, and calm. Proper socialization of your dog is a crucial part of preparing them for the rest of their life.

Exposure to the many things we take as normal, our little puppies and adult dogs do not. Mechanical noises such as appliances, lawnmowers, car horns, blenders, coffee machines, dishwashers, stereos, televisions, and other similar items are all noises that dogs have to adjust too. Beyond mechanical noises are living creatures, which represents other household pets, neighbor's dogs, and critters in the yard such as gophers, rabbits, squirrels, birds, family members, friends, neighbors, and of course the imposing stranger.

All of these are new to most eight-week-old puppies arriving at your house. Immediate gradual introduction to these machines, noises, and living creatures begins from day one. Always be alert to your puppy's reactions and willingness to either dive forward or withdrawal, and never force him or her to interact with things they do not wish too. Proceed at their pace by presenting the interaction and then observing their willingness of participation. When strangers approach your dog do not allow them to automatically reach out and touch, leave a little space and time for your puppy's reaction to be observed, and then you can grant or deny permission based upon you and your puppy's intuition.

Socialization Summary Goals

- Learning to remain calm when the world is buzzing around them.

- Exposure in a safe manner to the environment that will encompass his or her world, including the rules and guidelines that accompany it.

- Learning to respond to signals when they do not want too. For example, in the midst of a chasing session with another puppy, or an irresistible squirrel.

The first phase of socialization begins as early as 3 weeks and lasts to approximately 12 weeks old, during this time puppies discover that they are dogs and begin to play with their littermates. Survival techniques that they will use throughout their lives, such as biting, barking, chasing, and fighting, begin to be acted out. Concurrently during this time-period, puppies experience big changes socially and physically. Learning submissive postures and taking corrections from their mother, interaction with their littermates begin to teach them about hierarchies. Keeping mother and puppies together for at least 7-8 weeks tends to increase their ability to get along well with other dogs and learn more about themselves and their actions, such as the force of a bite on their brothers and sisters.

Keep your puppy out of harm's way when he is little. During this time, he can easily pick up diseases from sniffing other dog's feces and urine. When you are first exposing your puppy to new living creatures and places, it is good practice to carry him to and from the car. Follow this practice when near any dog clinics, both inside and outside. Keeping your pup protected from contaminated ground surfaces will help keep him healthy. Until he has had his vaccines, and is a bit older, avoid areas where you suspect other dogs might have eliminated.

Between the ages of 7-12 weeks, a period of rapid learning occurs and they learn what humans are, and whether to accept them as safe. This is a crucial period, and has the *greatest impact* on *all future social behavior.*

This is the time we begin teaching puppies the acceptable rules of conduct. Take note that they have a short attention span, and physical limitations. This is the easiest period to get your puppy comfortable with new things, and the chance to thwart later behavioral issues that stem from improper or incomplete socialization. Puppies are not out of harm's way from all diseases at this time, but the risk is relatively low because of primary vaccines, good care, and mother's milk immunity. Behavioral problems are the greatest threat to the owner-dog bond and the number one cause of death to dogs under 3 years of age.

Enrolling your puppy in classes before 3 months of age is an outstanding avenue to improving socialization, training, and strengthen the bond between you and your puppy.

NewPuppyStuff.com

You can begin socialization classes as early as 7-8 weeks. The recommendation is to have your puppy receive at least *one* set of vaccines, and a de-worming *seven* days prior to starting the first class.

From birth, puppies should be exposed to handling and manipulation of body parts, and exposure to different people, places, situations, well socialized animals, and more. Encourage your puppies exploring, curiosity, and investigation of different environments. Games, toys, and a variety of surfaces such as, tile, concrete, tunnels, and steps are all things to expose your puppy too and should continue into adulthood to keep your dog sociable and not shy.

It is important for your puppy to be comfortable playing, sleeping, or exploring alone. Schedule alone play with toys, and solo naps in their crate or another safe area. This teaches them to entertain themselves and not become overly attached, or have separation issues with their owners. Getting them comfortable with their crate is also beneficial for travel and to use as a safe area for your puppy to relax.

Two phases of fear imprinting occur in your growing puppy's life. *A fear period is a stage during which your puppy or dog may be more apt to perceive certain stimuli as threatening.*

During these two periods, any event your puppy thinks is traumatic can leave a lasting effect, possibly forever. The first period is from 8-11 weeks and the second is between 6-14 months of age. During these periods, you will want to keep your puppy clear of any frightening situations, but

NewPuppyStuff.com

that is not always easy to determine. A chrome balloon on the floor could possibly severely frighten your little pup. There is no one size fits all in knowing what is fearful for your puppy. Becoming familiar with canine body language can help you diagnose your pups fear factor. The second period often reflects the dog becoming more reactive or apprehensive about new things. Larger breeds sometimes have an extended second period.

Keep a few things in mind when seeking play dates for socialization of your puppy. A stellar puppy class will have a safe, mature dog for the puppies to learn boundaries and other behaviors. When making play dates, puppies should be matched by personality and play styles. Games, such as retrieve or drop, help to curb possessive behaviors, as well as to help them learn to give up unsafe or off limits items, so that the item can be taken out of harm's way. Another important lesson during play is for puppies to learn to break away from playing and come back to their human. *Your dog should be willingly dependent upon you and look to you for guidance.*

Teach mature easily stimulated dogs to relax before they are permitted to socialize with others. If you have an adult dog that enjoys flying solo, do not force them into situations. Teach your dogs and puppies less aroused play and encourage passive play. This includes play that does not encompass dominance, mouthing, or biting other puppies. If you have rough play happening between multiple dogs or puppies, then interrupt the rough housing by frequently calling them to you and rewarding their attention. The attention then is turned to you. As a distraction to dissuade mouthing contact, try to interject toys into the play. Elevated play can lead to aggression as they grow, especially breeds that can easily get to full arousal in seconds.

Proper socialization requires patience, kindness, and consistency while teaching. You and your dog should both be having fun during this process. Allow your dog to proceed into new situations at his or her own pace, never force them into a situation that they are not comfortable. If you think that your dog may have a socialization issue, seek professional advice from a qualified behavioral person.

Socializing your puppy, especially before the age of six months, is a very important step in preventing future behavioral problems. Socializing can and should continue throughout the lifetime of your dog. Socializing in a gentle and kind manner prevents aggressive, fearful, and potential behaviors that affect humans. A lack of socializing may lead to *fear*, *aggression*, *barking*, shyness, *destruction*, territorialism, or *hyperactivity*.

The earlier you begin socializing, the better. However, all puppies and dogs can gradually be brought into new and initially frightening situations, eventually learning to enjoy them. Canines can adapt to various and sometimes extreme situations, they just need your calm, guiding hand.

Expect that the socializing of your dog will be a lifelong endeavor. If your puppy does not engage with other dogs for months or years at a time, you can expect his behavior to be different when he encounters them again.

Methods that can be used when exposing your dog to something new, or something he has previously been distrustful contacting.

- Remain calm, upbeat and if he has a leash on, keep it loose.

- Gradually expose him to the new stimulus and if he is wary or fearful never use force. Let him retreat if he needs to.

- Reward your dog using treats; give him a good scratch or an energetic run for being calm and exploring new situations.

Try on a regular basis to expose your dog to the things that you would like him to be capable to cope. His gained familiarity will allow him to calmly deal with such situations in the future. Be careful of the same old-same old. Though dogs love routine, periodically expose your dog to new things. This allows you to assess his need for further socialization. You certainly wouldn't want to go on vacation to the same place every single year, so why would he.

Examples of situations that benefit the social temperament of your dog.

- Meeting new kinds of people, including but not limited to, children, crowds, people wearing hats, disabled folks, and people in local services such as postal carriers, fire and police officers, and more. *"Introducing your puppy to a circus clown is saved for another chapter."*

- Meeting new dogs is encouraged. Because of canine diseases, be aware that you should wait at least 4 months before introducing your puppy to dog parks or places where there are groups of adult dogs. You can begin puppy socialization classes at around 7 weeks, just be sure your puppy has a round of vaccines at least a week prior. Slowly expose your dog to other pets, such as cats, horses, birds, llamas, pigs, gerbils, and monitor lizards.

- Your dog's crate is not a jail. Be sure and take the time to teach your puppy to enjoy the comfort and privacy of his own crate. You want your dog's crate to be a place that he or she feels safe.

Socialization Checklist

- To avoid doggy boredom, make sure you have plenty of toys for your dog to choose from out of the toy bin. A Nylabone®, a Kong®, dog chews, ropes, balls, and tugs are many of the popular things your dog can enjoy.

Be sure your dog is comfortable with the following:

- Human male and female adults.

- Human male and female children.

- Other household pets and dogs.

- Meeting strange dogs.

- Your house and neighborhood.

- Mechanical noises, such as lawn mowers and vehicles.

- Special circumstance people, for example, those in wheel chairs, with crutches, braces, or even strange family members.

To assure that your dog is not selfish, make sure that he or she is comfortable sharing the following:

- His food bowl, toys or bed being touched by you or others.

- The immediate space with strangers, especially with children. This is necessary for your puppy's socialization so that he does not get paranoid or freak out in small places. For example, elevators in Hollywood filled with celebrities or at the next-door neighbor's house.

- His best friend, YOU, and all family members and friends and is NOT overprotective or territorial.

For road tripping with your dog, make sure he or she is:

- Comfortable in all vehicles, such as a car, truck, minivan, or in a form of public transportation.

- Always properly restrained.

- You stop for elimination breaks and hydration.

- *Knows how to operate a stick shift as well as an automatic.*

In general, a happy puppy should have the following:

- You should provide at least 10 hours of sleep per night for your dog. This should occur in one of the household's adult bedrooms, but not in your bed. He or she should have their own bed or mat available to them.

- Regular health checks at the veterinarian are essential. He or she should receive at least the basic vaccinations, which includes rabies and distemper. Read up before agreeing on extra vaccinations and avoid unnecessary vaccinations or parasite treatments.

- Unless you are going to breed your dog, it is necessary that they be neutered or spayed.

- Maintain a proper weight for your dog. You should be able to feel his ribs but they do not stick out. He or she will have their weight checked at the vet and this will inform you on your dog's optimal weight.

- Plenty of playtime outside with proper supervision.

- It is essential that your dog have daily long walks, play, sport, or games.

The Importance of Play

When observing dogs in a pack or family, one will notice that dogs and puppies often enjoy playing with one another. During play puppies learn proper play etiquette, such as how hard to bite or mouth, and how rough to play. His mother and littermates provide feedback for him to assist in this learning. Play is instinctual, and as an innate dog behavior, it is something that needs to be satisfied. Humans and dogs both play throughout their lifetime and many studies show that this social interaction is important for the mental and physical health of the individual.

Providing your dog with ample amounts of play through games, such as fetch, tug, or chase helps to satisfy their need for play, and assists in strengthening the bond between dog and owner. When guided in play, your dog will not only acquire the rules of play, but his physical and mental needs will be met during the activity.

One terrific bi-product of play is that it burns off dog's excess energy, and as a result, it helps keep negative behaviors from surfacing.

NewPuppyStuff.com

Dogs are naturally full of energy, and they need an outlet to avoid these potential negative behaviors, which includes chewing, digging, and barking. While these behaviors serve them well in the wild, when living with humans they can be a detriment to the harmony and success of the relationship

Handling Your Dog

Teaching your dog to be still, calm, and patient while he is being handled is a very important step in your relationship. When you master this one, it will make life easier for both of you when at home, and at the groomer or vet. Handling also helps when there is unwanted or accidental touching and especially when dealing with small children who love to handle dogs in all sorts of unusual and not so regular ways. This one will take patience and a few tricks to get started. Remember, that it is important to begin handling your new puppy immediately after you find each other and are living together.

The sooner your puppy accepts your touches and manipulations the easier life will be for the both of you. Handling is needed for grooming, bathing, lifting, affection, inspecting for ticks, fleas, and injuries.

Recognize that muzzles are not bad and do not hurt dogs. They can be an effective device and a great safety feature when your dog is learning to be handled. Easy cheese or peanut butter spread on the floor or on the refrigerator door can keep your puppy in place while he learns to be handled. If your puppy does not like to be handled, he will slowly learn to accept it.

You must practice this with your puppy for at least one to three minutes each day so that he becomes comfortable with being touched. All dogs are unique and therefore some will accept this easier and quicker than others will. Handling training will be a life-long process.

With all of the following exercises, follow these steps:

- Begin with short, non-intrusive gentle touching. *If your puppy is calm* and he is not trying to squirm away, use a word such as "good," "nice," or "yes," and give your pup a treat.

- If your puppy squirms, keep touching him but do not fight his movements, keeping your hand lightly on him while moving your hand with his squirms. Use your hand as though it were a suction cup and stuck to the place that you are touching. When he settles, treat him and remove your hand.

- Work from one second to ten seconds or more, gradually working your way up to touching for longer durations, such as 2,4,6,8 to 10 seconds.

- Do not go forward to another step until your puppy adapts, and enjoys the current step.

- *Do not* work these exercises more than a couple of minutes at a time. Overstimulation can cause your puppy stress. Continue slowly at your puppy's comfortable speed.

Handling the Body

Paws

It is a fact that most puppies do not like to have their paws touched. Proceed slowly with this exercise. The eventual goal is for your puppy to adore his paws being fondled. In the following exercises, any time your puppy does not squirm and try to get away, *click and treat* your pup. If he does squirm, stay with him using gentle contact, when your pup ceases wiggling, then *click and treat*, and release when he calms down. Each one of these steps will take a few days to complete and will require at least a dozen repetitions.

Confirm that you successfully complete each step and your puppy is at least tolerant of the contact before you go on to the next one.

- Do each step with all four paws, and remember to pause a minute between paws, allowing your pup to regain his composure.

- Pick up your puppy's paw and immediately click and treat. Repeat this five times and then continue forward by adding an additional one second each time you pick up his paw until ten seconds is reached.

Hold the paw for ten to twelve seconds with no struggling from your dog. Begin with two seconds then in different sessions work your way to twelve.

During holding the paw, begin adding the following.

- Hold the paw and move it around.

- Massage the paw.

- Pretend to trim the nails.

Side Note: Do not trim your dog's nails unless you are positively sure you know what you are doing. It is not easy and if you are not properly trained can cause extreme pain to your dog.

The Collar

Find a quiet, low distraction place to practice, grab treats, and put your puppy's collar on him.

- While gently restrained, touch your dog's collar underneath his chin, and then release him right away simultaneously clicking and treating him. Do this about ten times or until your puppy seems comfortable and relaxed with the process.

- Grab and hold the collar where it is under his chin and hold it for about 2 seconds, C/T, and repeat. Increase the amount of time until you have achieved about ten seconds of holding and your puppy remains calm. Click and treat after each elapsed amount of time. By increasing the hold time by 2 seconds, gradually work your way up to ten seconds of holding. This may take several days and sessions.

- Hold the collar under his chin and now give it a little tug. If he accepts this and does not resist, click and treat, and repeat. If he squirms, keep a gentle hold on the collar until he calms down, and then C/T and release him. Repeat this step until he is content with the procedure.

Now, switch to the top of the collar and repeat the whole progression again. Remember slowly increase the time held and the intensity of the tug.

You can pull or tug, but *do not jerk* your puppy's neck or head because this can cause injury and interfere with your outcome objectives of the training exercise. You can practice touching the collar while you are treating during training other tricks. Gently hold the bottom or top of the collar when you are giving your dog a treat reward for successfully completing a commanded behavior.

Mouth

- Gently touch your puppy's mouth, *click and treat*, and repeat ten times.

- Touch the side of your puppy's mouth and lift a lip to expose a tooth, *click and treat*, then release only after he stops resisting.

- Gently and slowly, lift the lip to expose more and more teeth on both sides of the mouth, and then open the mouth. Then release when he does not resist, *click and treat*. Be cautious with this one.

- Touch a tooth with a toothbrush, then work up to brushing your puppy's teeth for one to ten-seconds, and then later increase the time. Brushing your puppy's teeth is something you will be doing a few times weekly for the lifetime of your dog.

Ears

- Reach around the side of your puppy's head, and then briefly and gently touch his ear. Click and treat, repeat ten times.

- When your puppy is comfortable with this, continue and practice holding the ear for one-second. If he is calm, click and treat. If he squirms, stay with him until he is calm. When your puppy calms down, click and treat, then release the ear. Do this until ten seconds is completed with no wiggling.

- Maneuver your pup's ear and pretend that you are cleaning it. Do this gently and slowly so that your puppy learns to enjoy it. It will take a few days of practice until your puppy is calm enough for the real ear cleaning. If your puppy is already sensitive about his ears being touched, it will take longer. See ear cleaning in the Basic Care section.

Proceed slowly at your puppy's comfortable pace. There is no rush just the end goal of your pup enjoying being handled in all sorts of ways that are beneficial to him.

Tail

Many puppies are sensitive about having their tails handled, and rightly so. Think about if someone grabs you by the arm and you are not fully ready. That is similar to the reaction a puppy feels when grabbed, especially when their tails are handled.

- Start by briefly touching his tail. When moving to touch your puppy's tail move slowly and let your hand be seen moving towards his tail. This keeps your puppy from being startled. Repeat this ten times with clicking and treating, until you notice your puppy is comfortable with his tail being touched.

- Increase the duration of time you hold his tail until you achieve the ten-second mark.

- Tenderly and cautiously, pull the tail up, brush the tail, and then tenderly pull on it until your dog allows you to do this without reacting by jerking, wiggling, or whimpering.

Children

You must prepare your poor puppy to deal with the strange, unwelcome touching that is often exacted on them by children. Alternatively, you could just put a sign around his neck that says; "You must be at least 16 to touch this puppy." However, it is very likely that your puppy will encounter children that are touchy, grabby, or pokey.

- Prepare your puppy for the strange touches that children may perpetrate by practicing while clicking and treating him for accepting these odd bits of contact such as ear tugs, tail tugs, and perhaps a little harder than usual head pats, kisses, and hugs. Keep in mind, as previously mentioned, puppies and kids are not a natural pairing, *but cheese and wine are*. Even a puppy that is *good with kids* can be pushed to a breaking point and then things can get ugly, and nobody wants that.

Always supervise children around your dog. ALWAYS! – It is a dog ownership law.

Can you give me a lift?

An emergency may arise that requires you to pick up your dog. As you do these maneuvers, move and proceed slowly and cautiously. First, briefly put your arms around your dog and then give him a click and treat if he stays still. Increase the time duration with successive repetitions. Your dog should be comfortable for ten to fifteen seconds with your arms around him. Next, slowly proceed lifting your dog off the ground just a few inches or centimeters, and then back down. Each time he does not wriggle, click and treat. Increase the time and the distance that you lift him from the ground and then move your dog from one place to another. Calculate the time it might take to lift and carry your dog from the house and place him into your vehicle. This is a good time goal to set for carrying your dog.

Eventually, by lifting your dog up and placing him on a table, you will be able to prepare your dog for trips to the groomer, open spaces, or the vet. If you own an extra-large dog, or dog that is too heavy for you to lift, solicit help for this training from family or a friend. *Gigantor* may take two to lift safely and properly, or use one of the methods below.

Once up on the table you can practice handling in ways a groomer or veterinarian might handle your dog. This is good preparation for a day at the dog spa or veterinary procedures.

How to lift a dog

To lift a large dog properly, always start by approaching the dog from the side. Place one of your hands upon the dog's rear end with the tail in the down position, unless it is a curly tailed spitz type dog that will not enjoy having its tail forced down. This protects the dog's tail from being forced painfully upwards should your arm slip.

You should be holding your dog directly underneath the dog's rear hips. Your other hand should be in the front of the dog around his front legs with your arm across his chest. Now your arms should be on your dog's chest and butt area. Then gently press your arms together as in a cradling position and lift using your legs. The human's body position should be that of having bent legs and crouching down so that the power in the legs is used to lift you and your dog upright. To prevent injury to yourself, keep your back as straight as possible.

Small dogs are simpler to lift and require much less effort, but still take great care not to inadvertently injure them.

Place your hand in between the back and front legs underneath the dog's underbelly. Supporting the rear with your forearm, additionally placing a hand on the dog's chest is a good idea for safety in the event that your dog squirms when being lifted.

For extra-large or dogs that are too heavy for you to lift, purchase and utilize a ramp so that your dog can walk itself into your vehicle. This saves you and your dog from possible or inevitable injury. It is always best to use caution instead of risking a painful, costly, or permanent injury. Of course, you can also teach your dog to jump into the vehicle. Later when your dog becomes aged, you can then utilize the ramp.

Some large dogs can be taught to put their front paws up onto the vehicle floorboard or tailgate, thus allowing you to help push them from their buttocks and assist them jumping in your vehicle.

Never grab, pull, or lift a dog by its fore or rear legs. This can cause serious pain and injury to a dog.

Brushing

- Get your puppy's brush and lightly touch him with it all over his body. If he remains unmoving, give him a click and treat, then repeat. Repeat this until you can brush every part of his body without him moving.

Your puppy will become comfortable with all varieties of touching and handling if you work slowly, patiently, and with plenty of good treats. Handling training is a very important step in your dog's socialization.

Giving Treats

Treats, treats, *treats!* "Come and get 'em." How many times have you heard a friend or family member tell you about some crazy food that their dog loves? Dogs do love a massive variety of foods; unfortunately, not all of the foods that they think they want to eat are good for them. Dog treating is not rocket science but it does take a little research, common sense, and paying attention to how your dog reacts after wolfing down a treat.

I am going to throw out some ideas for treats for training as well as some regular ole "Good Dog" treats for your sidekick and friend in mischief. I will touch on the proper time to treat, the act of giving the treat, types of treats, and bribery vs. reward.

Types of Treats

Love and attention is considered a reward and is certainly a positive reinforcement that can be just as effective as an edible treat. Dog treating is comprised of edibles, praise, love, and attention. Engaging in play or allowing some quality time with their favorite piece of rawhide is also effectual. At times, these treats are crucial to dog training.

Human foods that are safe for dogs, include most fruits and veggies, cut up meats that are raw or cooked, yogurt, peanut butter, kibble, and whatever else you discover that your dog likes, but be sure that it is good for him, in particular his digestive system. Remember, not all human foods are good for dogs. Please read up on the dos and don'ts regarding human foods and dogs. A "treat" is considered something about the size of a kernel of corn. All a dog needs is a little taste to keep him interested. The kernel size is something that is swiftly eaten and swallowed, making it non-distracting from training. Remember, a treat is just quick tasted, used for enticement and reinforcement.

Giving the Treat

Try to avoid treating your dog when he is over stimulated and running amuck in an unfocused state of mind. This can be counterproductive and might reinforce a negative behavior resulting in you not being able to get your dog's attention.

When giving the treat, allow your dog to get a big doggie whiff of that nibble of tasty food treat, but keep it up and away from a possible attempt at a quick snatch and grab. Due to their keen sense of smell, they will know long before you figure it out that there is a tasty snack nearby.

Issue your command and wait for him to obey before presenting the doggie reward. Remember that when dog treating, it is important to be patient and loving, but it is equally important not to give the treat until he obeys. Try to use treating to reward the kickback mellow dog, not the out of control or over-excited dog.

Some dogs have a natural gentleness to them and always take from your hand gently, while other dogs need some guidance to achieve this. If your dog is a bit rough during treat grabbing, go ahead and train the command "gentle!"

when giving treats. Be firm from this point forward. Give up no treats unless taken gently. Be steadfast with your decision to implement this, because if he wants the tasty treat, he will soon comply.

Time to Treat

The best time to be issuing dog treats is in between his or her meals. During training, always keep the tastiest treat in reserve in case you need to gain your dog's attention back to the current training session.

It is good to keep in mind that treating too close to meal times makes all treats less effective, so remember this when planning your training sessions. Obviously, if your dog is full from mealtime he will be less likely to want a treat reward than if he is a bit hungry, therefore your training session will likely be more difficult and far less effective.

What's In the Treats?

Before purchasing, look at the ingredients on the treat packaging, and make certain there are no chemicals, fillers, additives, colors and things that are unhealthy. Certain human foods that are tasty to us might not be so tasty to your dog, and he will tell you. Almost all dogs love some type of raw or cooked meats. In tiny nibble sizes (size of a corn kernel), these treats work great to get their attention where you want it focused.

Many people like to make homemade treats and that is fine, just keep to the rules we just mentioned and watch what you are adding while you are having fun in the kitchen.

NewPuppyStuff.com

Remember to research and read the list of vegetables dogs can and cannot eat, and note that pits and seeds can cause choking and intestinal issues, such as dreaded doggy flatulence. Remove the seeds and pits, and clean all fruits and veggies before slicing it into doggie size treats.

Bribery vs. Reward Dog Treating

The other day a friend of mine mentioned *bribery* for an action when he wanted his dog to shake his hand. I thought about it later and thought I would clarify for my readers. *Bribery* is the act of offering the food in advance to get the dog to act out a command or behavior. *Reward* is giving your dog his favorite toy, food, love, affection *after* he has performed the behavior.

An example of bribery would be, if you want your dog to come and you hold out in front of you in your hand a huge slab of steak before calling him. Reward would be giving your dog the steak after he obeyed the "come!" command.

Bribed dogs learn to comply with your wishes only when they *see* food. The rewarded dog realizes that he only gets his reward after performing the desired action. This also assists by introducing non-food items as rewards when training and treating. Rewards such as play, toys, affection, and praise can be substituted for treats.

"Thank you for reading, "Don't Think, BE – Alpha Dog - Alpha Dog Secrets."

We know that you will make a great trainer, owner, and friend to your dog or puppy. Throughout the lifetime of your friendship, be firm but fair, patient and loving."

~ Paps ~

Health Insurance for my Dog?
Really? Why?

Because Paying Cash Makes No "Cents" or Does It?
Shocking Statistics! **Discover the Truth!**

healthypaws
PET INSURANCE & FOUNDATION

Protect Your Pet.
Save a Homeless Pet.

TRUSTED BY PET PARENTS & LOVED BY PETS!

Protect your best friend and save on vet bills!

- ✓ Lifetime discounts up to 10%
- ✓ Unlimited Benefits
- ✓ #1 Customer-Rated Plan

Quote and Save

~ Type Into Your Browser

nobrainerdogtrainer.com/insurance-for-dogs/

NewPuppyStuff.com

Hey...Did I miss something?

STUMPED?

Got a Question about Your Dog?

Ask an Expert Now!

Facebook

facebook.com/Newdogtimes-866887790092493

NewDogTimes ~ newdogtimes.com

*It's where the **Dog Secrets** have been hidden -since their Ancestral Wolf Packs were forced to collide with Man...*

Wait Until You Learn This

NewPuppyStuff.com

About the Author

Paul Allen Pearce is the author of many breed specific dog-training books.

As a youth, a family trip to Australia forever changed the course Paul would take on his way to return home to South Carolina to begin a family, raise dogs, and eventually write. For a year in high school, Paul headed back to Australia to study, and then again, during college he did the same.

Paul's family is dog lovers and often took in strays. Paul and his siblings were taught how to care and train the family pets and dogs. Both his parents grew up with many animals and had generational knowledge to pass forth to their offspring. Being reared around all sorts of animals, his curiosity to work with animals grew. Upon returning back to the U.S. and purchasing his own dog he realized he didn't know as much as he could, thus began his journey into owning and full time dog training.

Paul states, "Dog training is my passion. I love dogs, animals, and the wonders of nature. It is easy to write about your passion and share what you have learned and discovered. I hope that my readers enjoy and learn from what I have learned and improve their dog relationships.

My past explorations throughout twenty countries and states helped me to broaden my perspective regarding animal behavior and treatment. Let us all be kind to animals, not only dogs."

NewPuppyStuff.com

Other Books

"No Brainer Dog Trainer"
(Breed specific dog training series)

"Think Like a Dog…but don't eat your poop!"
(Breed specific dog training series)

"Think Like Me…but don't eat your poop!
(Breed specific dog training series)

NewPuppyStuff.com

NewPuppyStuff.com

Content Attributions

Photos: We wish to thank all of the photographers for sharing their photographs via Creative Commons Licensing.

Flickr - Wiki commons

Cover Image Free License Agreement:

File: #77897576 | Author: erika8213
https://us.fotolia.com/Info/Agreements/StandardLicense

Treats -
http://upload.wikimedia.org/wikipedia/commons/e/ef/Treats-IMGP9845-1.jpg,By Stacy Lynn Baum (Stacy Lynn Baum) [CC-BY-3.0 (http://creativecommons.org/licenses/by/3.0)], via Wikimedia Commons, No changes were made. Plus stock photo's.

Legal Disclaimer:

The author of "Don't Think, BE – Alpha Dog", Paul Allen Pearce is in no way responsible at any time for the action of your pet, not now or in the future. Animals, without warning, may cause injury to humans and/or other animals. Paul Allen Pearce is not responsible for attacks, bites, mauling', nor any other viciousness or any and all other damages. We strongly recommend that you exercise caution for the safety of self, the animal, and all around the animals while working with your dog. We are not liable for any animal or human medical conditions or results obtained from training. While all attempts have been made to verify information provided in this publication, neither the author nor the publisher assume any responsibility for errors, omissions or contrary interpretation of the subject matter contained herein. The publisher and author assume no responsibility or liability whatsoever on the behalf of any purchaser or reader of the material provided.

NewPuppyStuff.com

Printed in Great Britain
by Amazon